Iowa's Tradition

An

ABC

Photo Album

of the

Iowa State Fair

By J.O. Parker and Debbie Tindle Parker

Our Front Porch Books
Montezuma, Iowa USA

Copyright © 2006 by J.O. and Debbie Parker

Library of Congress Control Number: 2006927092

ISBN-13: 978-0-9786931-0-7
ISBN-10: 0-9786931-0-8

Published by:
Our Front Porch Books
P.O. Box 902
Montezuma, Iowa 50171
(641) 990-0953

www.ourfrontporchbooks.com

Printed by:
Sutherland Printing
525 North Front Street
Montezuma, Iowa 50171
(641) 623-5115

www.sutherlandprinting.com

Our Front Porch Books

First Edition - First Printing

Canon EOS-1N and Konica FT1 cameras and Fujicolor Superia Reala 100 film were used to produce this book.

This book
is dedicated
to those who
hold the Iowa
State Fair near
and dear to
their hearts
- whether you
dream about
childhood
memories, plan
to visit, or
faithfully
attend
every year
— this book is
for you.

Iowa State Fair Facts

• The first Iowa State Fair was held in Fairfield in 1854 and moved to the present site in Des Moines in 1886.

• The budget for the first Iowa State Fair in 1854 was $323.

• The fairgrounds are made up of approximately 400 acres, which includes a 160-acre campground.

• What takes approximately 550 pounds of butter and 16 hours to craft?
Iowan Duffy Lyon's Butter Cow sculpture, which is exhibited in a 40-degree showcase cooler in the Agriculture Building. Butter sculpture has been part of the Fair since 1911.
— Fun fact: Phil Stong, author of the famous novel *State Fair*, is butter sculptor Duffy Lyon's uncle.

• The hottest temperature ever recorded at the fair was 108 degrees on Older Iowans' Day, Aug. 16, 1983.

• There are more than 20 types of food that can be purchased "on-a-stick" at the fair. The list includes: pork chops, dill pickles, fried pickles, cheese, Cajun chicken, chocolate cheesecake, hot bologna, chocolate covered bananas, taffy, honey, wonder bars, deep fried Twinkies, meatballs, Ho-Hos and fudge puppies (waffles drenched in chocolate sauce).

• Approximately how many pork chops do the Iowa Pork Producers sell during a Fair?

Pork lovers gobble down approximately 5,000 to 6,000 chops daily during the Fair's 11-day run. In 2003, the Pork Producers served their one-millionth customer.

• Who holds the record for attracting the largest Grandstand crowd?
In 1972 Sonny and Cher attracted 26,200 in two shows. In 1975 the Beach Boys drew 25,400 in one show. In 1970 Johnny Cash attracted 25,300 in two shows. In 1974 Chicago played to 24,700 in one show. In 1982 the Oak Ridge Boys drew 23,500 in two shows.

• Which United States presidents have visited the State Fair?
Herbert Hoover, Dwight Eisenhower, Gerald Ford, Jimmy Carter and George W. Bush. Ronald Reagan broadcast from the Fair as sports director for WHO radio in the 1930s.

• Members of the Iowa State Fair Board are elected annually by delegates from Iowa's 106 county fairs.

• Chainsaw carver Brian Ruth crafted five stunning wood sculptures from what naturally occurring materials on the Fairgrounds in 1998?
Storm-damaged trees.

• What's the origin of Grandfather's Barn?
The barn was part of the original farmstead purchased in 1886 by the State of Iowa for the Fair's permanent home.

• The first Hog Calling competition at the Iowa State Fair was held in 1926.

• What happens to the animal bedding following the Fair?
An average 1,600 tons of bedding is applied to several hundred acres of farm land.

• When did the original State Fair Museum open?
The museum, located across from Pioneer Hall, opened in 1982.

• Since 1993, the Blue Ribbon Foundation has worked to raise the funds needed to restore the Fair's buildings and grounds. More than $50 million has been raised, pledged or committed and numerous projects completed to date. More than two-thirds of that total has been appropriated by the Iowa legislature.

• A few of the nationally known magazines who have covered the fair are: The National Geographic Traveler, Cosmopolitan, Time, Life, ESPN Magazine, Newsweek, People, Midwest Living and Better Homes and Gardens.

• If you unrolled all the toilet tissue stockpiled for the Fair, how many miles would it stretch?
1,818 miles (That's 5 trips to Chicago from Des Moines, or one trip to Los Angeles!)

Source: Iowa State Fair

Introduction

Photo albums are the keepers of memories that you take off the shelf to relive special, unforgettable moments. For more than 150 years, visitors of all ages have been making memories while enjoying the Iowa State Fair. And during that long history, the fair has gained worldwide attention yet has been able to maintain its charmful simplicity.

This book is full of memories from the 2005 Iowa State Fair; however, all the pictures contain items that you can see any year that you have attended or will be attending the fair. Although certain acts may not be present, there are always entertainers gracing the fairgrounds. Certain food stands may come and go, but there is always delicious food around every bend. And contests change, but the determination, drive and desire to do your best is always in style.

Grab an ice cold drink, sit back and enjoy a few snapshots of Iowa's Tradition - the Iowa State Fair.

"We hope you get as much enjoyment from reading this book as we did creating it."

— J.O. and Debbie

A

APPLES

Blue Ribbon **APPLE** winners are displayed in the main level of the Agriculture Building. Fruit crop classes are open to all Iowa growers, including commercial and amateur. Judges award points based on form, size, uniformity, color and condition, which is the most important. Fruit cannot be waxed, polished or otherwise treated or it will be disqualified.

ARM WRESTLING

Bobby Chance of Cambridge, Iowa and Scott Mineart of Earlham, Iowa compete in the 27th annual Monster **ARM** Wrestling competition, which is held in the Penningroth Media Center in the cattle barn. April Brubaker of Le Grand, Iowa and Harriett Hull of Quarry, Iowa insure that all the rules are being followed during the match. Bobby, who has been participating in arm wrestling events for 9 years, went on to win 2nd place in both the left and right middleweight competitions. There were 81 men and women who competed.

BELLY DANCING

Ilima (her dance name) teaches Taylor Young, age 7, of Des Moines, Iowa how to **BELLY** dance on the Anderson Erickson KCCI NewsChannel 8 Stage. Ilima is part of the Mirage Middle Eastern Belly Dancing Troupe. The group has been entertaining for 20 years and is based in Central Iowa. Their goal is to teach others the art of Middle Eastern dance and they perform at various cultural events and art festivals.

B

<u>BOOTS</u>

Stands are scattered around and throughout the livestock barns offering **BOOTS** and other western wear
and animal care items.

C

<u>CORNDOGS</u>

This couple enjoys one of the fair's famous foods – **CORNDOGS**.

Photos at Right: An unique competition, the **COW CHIP** throwing contest, is held on the west side of Pioneer Hall every year. The competition attracts more than 200 competitors, and a large group of spectators, who often have to duck to avoid the flying cow pies. Pictured (middle) is Sara Alexander of Brooklyn, Iowa tossing the cow chip. Sara was in the ladies division. There are also divisions for men, children and celebrities. (Right) Jacob Suchanek, 12, of Tama, Iowa gathers the cow chips after they are thrown and their distance has been measured by Ronald West of Baxter, Iowa. (Top left) A female competitor gets the feel of her chosen cow chip, while she ponders her throwing technique on the rocky hill.

COW CHIP THROWING CONTEST

PIONEER HALL

D

<u>DOMINOS</u>

Scott Suko of Dayton, Maryland prepares his **DOMINOS** for the daily domino toppling that took place on the lower level of the Cultural Center in 2005. Scott spent 10 hours each day setting up 6,000 dominos in preparation for the big moment. Often the entertainment showcased at the Cultural Center changes yearly.

<u>DOLLS</u>

These beautiful **DOLLS** were anxiously waiting to be purchased in the Buckskinners' Rendezvous Camp.

<u>EXPERTS</u>

The Iowa State Fair food department is the largest in the nation. Prizes of around $60,000 are awarded in nearly 900 classes with almost 14,000 entries. Joan Slotten of West Des Moines, Iowa and Nancy Mathieson, membership coordinator of the American Pie Council (APC) from Lake Forest, Illinois provided their **EXPERT** skills as pie judges. Other categories included cinnamon rolls, cookies and graham cracker/gingerbread houses.

E

ELEPHANT EARS

A deep-fried, cinnamon dessert - **ELEPHANT EARS** - was a popular choice
for the hungry fairgoer who deserved a rich treat after walking for miles.

F

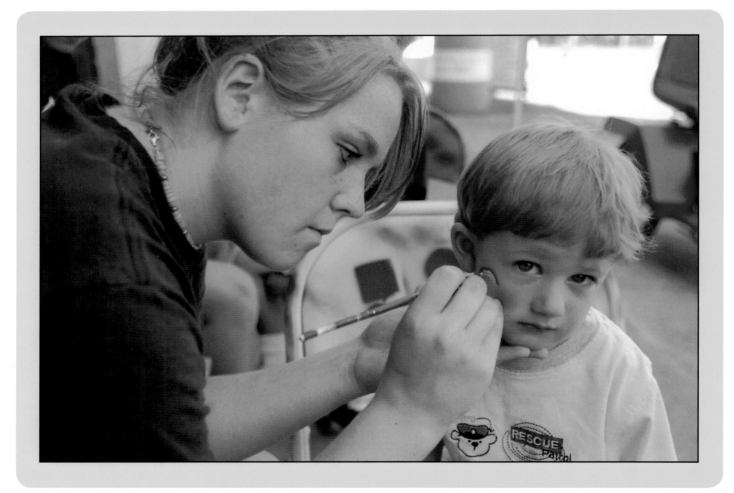

<u>FACE PAINTING</u>

Gavin Tindle, 2 1/2, of Montezuma, Iowa concentrates while having his **FACE** paint-
ed by Rachel Howieson, a student at Carlisle High School. Rachel works with Inno-
vativevents Inc., a Des Moines-based family-owned company that has been offering
artistic creations on the north side of the Cultural Center for the past 17 years.

<u>FISH</u>

Four young fairgoers enjoy examining a variety of **FISH** found in Iowa's lakes and streams. The display is in the Iowa Department of Natural Resources Building located just west of the Grandstand.

G

<u>GIANT</u> <u>SLIDE</u>

Chris Hook of Earlham, Iowa and Stacey Mercer of West Des Moines, Iowa enjoy a ride down the **GIANT SLIDE**. A yearly trip down the Giant Slide is a must for many long-time fair attendees.

The Dancin' **GRANNIES** from the Trinity United Methodist Church in Albia, Iowa took home the Grand Championship title from the Older Iowan's Day Music Competition, after a first place finish in the dance competition. Other categories included vocal, instrumental and kitchen band. The group, which has been performing for 14 years, was founded by Nancy Henderson and consists of women, ranging in age from 60 to 85. They practice twice a week and perform around 80 times per year at fairs, banquets and nursing homes.

The Dancin' GRANNIES

HONEY COMPETITION

These top winning **HONEY** 'bears' stand at attention on the top floor of the Agriculture Building. Entered in the Plastic Bear competition of the Apiary (Bees & Honey) Department, entries consisted of six 12 oz. plastic bears of honey. The honey must be the product of the exhibitor's apiary. In this category, judges took into consideration the condition of the container, flavor, color and clarity of honey, moisture content, uniform volume of honey in all of the containers and freedom from impurities including foam and granulation. Those who scored highest out of 100 points received ribbons and premiums ranging from $8 - $20.

H

HATCHET

Snake, who is part of the Buckskin-ners' Rendezvous Camp, examines his **HATCHET** throw. He took audience members on a journey of mountain man life during daily shows. Snake is from Monroe, Iowa.

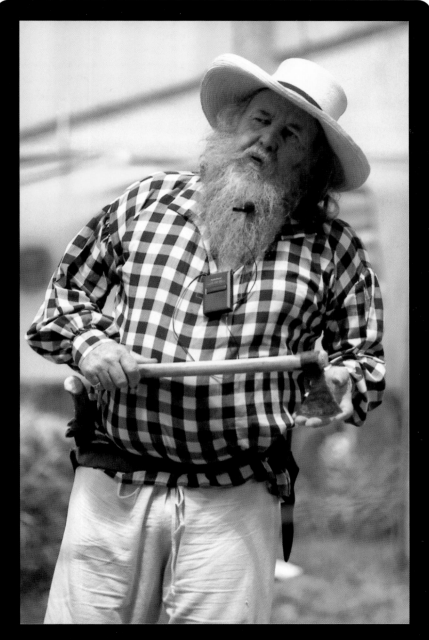

I

INTERVIEW

Steve Karlin, anchorman on KCCI NewsChannel 8's First News at Five, clowns around during his **INTERVIEW** with **IOWA** Public Television. Steve was part of the KCCI NewsChannel 8 Umbrella of Protection team, which won the 2005 Outhouse Races and was awarded $100 and a golden throne inscribed "You're Number 1 in the Number 2 Business".

ICE CREAM

Hungry, hot fairgoers are often on the prowl for something cool and delicious. Linda Jones of New Virginia, Iowa scoops up generous cones at the **ICE CREAM** shop along Grand Avenue by the General Store. The giant **ICE CREAM** cone on the right is sending out a beacon to weary tourists who are searching for a cool treat along the Grand Concourse.

J

<u>JUGGLING</u>

Dale Jones of St. Louis, Missouri was a strolling, one-arm, **JUGGLING** act at the fair. Due to an injury that occurred when he was 8 and resulted in the loss of use in his right arm, Dale had to come up with a new way of juggling. Dale was one of several acts that performed in different locations around the fairgrounds.

JUMBO PUMPKIN

Leonora Mae James, 5, of Carlisle, Iowa pales in size compared to the Iowa State Fair record-setting **JUMBO PUMPKIN**, which weighed in at 881.5 pounds, breaking the old record by 9.6 pounds. The jumbo pumpkin was grown by Mike Frantz of Walcott, Iowa. Look for jumbo pumpkins displayed in the Agriculture Building. While there, look for the jumbo watermelon, squash, muskmelon, cabbage, potatoes, tomatoes and apples.

<u>KIDS</u>

Aly James, 11, of Searsboro, Iowa has a quiet moment with her cow, Jazz. She and Jazz received a 3rd place finish in the Junior Iowa Red Angus Futurity competition at the 2005 Iowa State Fair. Aly was a busy **KID** at the fair. She also showed her dog in the 4-H dog show, participated in the Bill Riley Talent show (after qualifying at the local level) and danced in the 4-H dance review. Aly and her family stayed in the campgrounds.

K

And More...

<u>KIDS</u>

Top on **KIDS'** "To Do" lists at the fair is spending quality time running through the water fountains in the Pella Plaza. Secretly, it is on many adults' lists, too!

L

<u>LEMONADE</u>

Iowa summers can be brutally hot and a brim-full cup of ice cold **LEMONADE** is another fair-time favorite. There were at least 18 stands that offered the sweet treat.

LAMPS

These beautiful glass **LAMPS** were just some of the antiques for sale in Pioneer Hall. Also on display in Pioneer Hall are items entered in the Heritage Exhibits competition. Items have to be genuine and at least 50 years old. Reproductions are disqualified. Some of the classes include pottery, toys, books, christening gowns, sleigh bells and Iowa State Fair souvenirs. Award winners in the competition receive a ribbon and small premium. The items in the competitions are not offered for sale during the fair.

MOTORCYCLE

This sleek blue and chrome Harley **MOTORCYCLE** was on display along the Grand Concourse on Extreme Sunday. Look closely – can you see the tractor tram passing by in the distance? Turn to letter P for a hint or log on to: www.ourfrontporchbooks.com.

<u>MUSIC</u>

MUSIC is an important part of the fair. Many genres of music are offered on the free stages around the fairgrounds. One of the groups that provided free entertainment were the Fox Brothers, a comedy country gospel group from Bending Chestnut, Tennessee. Lead singer, Randy Fox, is accompanied by his son, Brent, on the trumpet. Brent is also the sound engineer for the group. Other family members in the group are Randy's brothers, Lynn and Roy.

N

NEON

Once the sun goes down, hungry fairgoers use **NEON** lights from food concession stands to locate their stomach's desire. There are approximately 200 food stands that offer a variety of treats including cotton candy, nut rolls and pork chops on a stick.

NAIL DRIVING CONTEST

Many women showed up to try their hand at the ladies **NAIL** driving contest that was held in Pioneer Hall. Contestants were trying to drive five nails flush within a small square marked on the board before putting down their hammers and raising their hands. More than 50 ladies competed.

Ready, Set,   GO - - -

OUTHOUSE RACES

Four businesses competed in the 2nd Annual **OUTHOUSE RACES** on the Grand Concourse. The teams constructed their own outhouses prior to the races. During the race, three members of the team push the outhouse while a fourth member drives. They race to a toilet where the driver cleans off the seat without using their hands. Then the driver searches for a corn cob buried in a cattle trough, puts a roll of toilet paper on a holder and returns to the outhouse before the team races back to the starting point. The KCCI NewsChannel 8 Umbrella of Protection team is the group to beat as they are the undefeated champions.

O

OSTRICH

A popular attraction among children is the petting zoo. This **OSTRICH** enjoys eating pet food out of a cup from a visitor. Pet food is available for purchase and admission to the petting zoo is free. Other animals that were at the zoo included zebras, goats and a kangaroo.

PORCH PICKING

Steve Ueding of Colfax, Iowa and Lori O'Hern of Des Moines, Iowa enjoy entertaining a crowd of resting fairgoers on the **PORCH** of the Old Museum by **PICKING** their instruments. They were accompanied by Lori's husband, Bob, and others and held impromptu performances in various locations around the fairgrounds. Steve also placed 2nd in the mandolin competition and 3rd in the guitar contest which were both part of the Rural Americana Olde Tyme Competitions held in Pioneer Hall.

P

PONY RIDE

Sixteen-month-old Sawyer Tindle of Montezuma, Iowa contemplates taking the reins as he enjoys a **PONY** ride outside of Grandfather's Farm. Passing by in the distance is the tram that carries visitors around the fairgrounds for free.

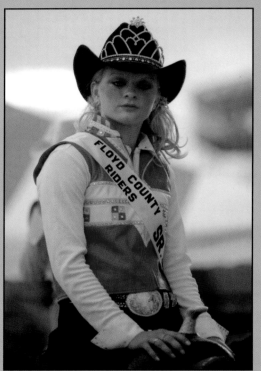

Photo at Far Left: The 2005 Iowa State Fair **QUEEN**, Stephanie Miller, 17, of Fayette enjoys a fun moment at the fair. Stephanie, who became eligible to participate in the queen competition after being crowned Fayette County Fair Queen in July, was one of 102 contestants who vied for the title. Stephanie was the first ever Fayette County Queen to become the Iowa State Fair Queen.

Photo at Left: Sarah Clarkson, a senior at Nora Springs High School, mentally prepares to participate in the Senior Division of the Cowgirl **QUEEN** Competition, held in the Livestock Pavilion. Sarah, a member of the Floyd County Riders, won at the county level to be eligible to participate at the fair.

Dara-Renée Hollinsed of New York, New York learns how to **QUILT** in one of the Fabrics and Threads Department's "Make It and Take It" classes offered upstairs in the Varied Industries Building. Maybe someday soon she will be able to make one like this Iowa State Fair **QUILT**.

QUILTING

R

<u>RABBIT</u>

Prizes are given for the largest animal in many classes including Biggest Boar, Ram, Bull, Heaviest Pigeon and Largest **RABBIT**. 'Gracie', who belongs to Dwight Westercamp of Batavia, Iowa was the 2005 Iowa State Fair Largest Rabbit, weighing in at 17 pounds, 13 ounces. It was the eighth consecutive win for Dwight's rabbits. The Iowa State Fair record for the largest rabbit was set in 1998 at 19 pounds and 6 ounces. The Largest Rabbit can be seen in the Pigeon, Poultry and Rabbit Building.

LARGEST RABBIT
BREED Flemish Giant
WEIGHT 17 lbs. 13 oz.
OWNER Mr.+Mrs. Dwight Westercamp
CITY, STATE Batavia, IA

KEEP FINGERS OUT
OF CAGES;
RABBITS
MIGHT BITE
MANTENGA DEDOS FUERA
de JAULAS; CONEJOS
QUIZAS MUERDAN.

RIBBONS

Mark Hiser of Butler, Indiana takes advantage of his down-time by resting under his display of **ROSETTES**. Mark shows horses owned by Shady Creek Percherons from New Haven, Indiana. Approximately 85,000 **RIBBONS**, rosettes and banners are awarded at the fair each year.

S

<u>SKYGLIDER</u>

Each year thousands of fair-goers enjoy a peaceful ride on the **SKYGLIDER**. There are two Skyglider rides and both offer spectacular views of the beautiful fairgrounds and all it has to offer.

<u>SHEEP</u>

Brent Ness and his fiancee, Jenny Hawkins, of Waterville, Iowa prepare **SUFFOLK SHEEP** for sale. Brent owns the sheep business along with his brother, Scott and their father, Sigurd. These sheep were sold during the Iowa Club lamb sale after being shown in open competition at the fair.

TICKET TAKER

Ruth Patience of Perry, Iowa takes **TICKETS** from anxious fairgoers entering the grounds at Gate 5, which is one of the gates that lead in from the 160 acre campground. Campers staying for the duration of the fair reserve their spots in advance. Those who only come for a day or two don't need reservations. Because of the popularity of the campgrounds, there is a waiting list for reserved spots.

T

TRACTOR PULLS

A participant in the **TRACTOR** pulls is preparing for his turn at the track. The tractor pulls were held in the Grandstand on the half-mile dirt track that has been the site for competitions since the early 1900s.

U

UGLY CAKE CONTEST

One of the kids' competitions in the food department is the **UGLY** cake contest sponsored by Chuck E. Cheese. Kids use edible items to make a very unappetizing treat. There are two classes, junior, ages 7-11 and intermediate, ages 12-17. Cakes are split into general and theme categories and are judged on appearance. If your stomach can handle it, you can view them in the Family Center.

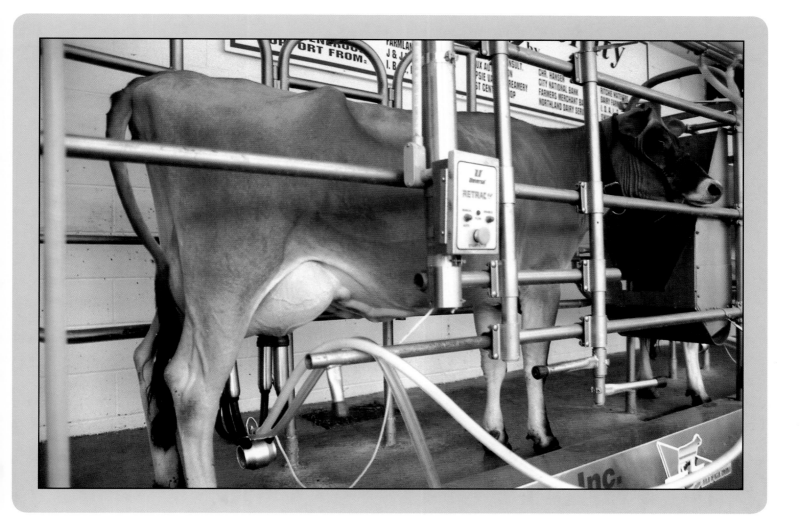

<u>UDDERS</u>

A delicious treat on a hot, Iowa day is ice cream. This cow was helping provide that sweet treat. Her **UDDERS** were hooked up to machines that collected her milk in the viewable, working milking parlor. Then her milk was mixed with other ingredients, which were used to make delicious ice cream. You can view the milking parlor on the north side of the cattle barn while waiting in line to purchase your own sample.

VOLUNTEERS

Hundreds of people **VOLUNTEER** their time to help out at the fair, both through the Blue Ribbon Foundation and though the Iowa State Fair. These two women were Blue Ribbon volunteers who sold merchandise in the Richard L. Easter Museum Complex, which opened in 2005. Foundation volunteers donate their time selling merchandise and bottled water and work in four-hour shifts. Fair volunteers donate their time staffing information booths, diaper-changing/nursing stations and the Little Hands on the Farm exhibit. For more information on being a volunteer log onto www.blueribbonfoundation.org or www.iowastatefair.org.

V

VARIED INDUSTRIES BUILDING

The **VARIED** Industries Building, built in 1911 and renovated in 2001, stands in the center of it all – along the Grand Concourse. During the fair, one can find everything from hot tubs and cookware to competing colleges and political parties. Offering a variety of vegetables - some on a stick - the **VEGGIE-TABLE** concession stand is located in front of the Varied Industries Building along the Grand Concourse.

W

<u>WEIGH-IN (GOAT MILK)</u>

Morgan Allen, 24, of Kenyon, Minnesota is waiting for the results of the goat milk **WEIGH-IN** competition. Morgan, along with her mother, Andrea Strusz, of Red Wing, Minnesota show goats at eight fairs per year. Morgan and Andrea got top milk producer honors in three different breed classes in which they competed.

<u>WATERMELON</u>

Al Wills of Altoona, Iowa works quickly to transform a whole **WATERMELON** into bite-sized chunks, which are available for purchase by the cup full.

"X" Section of the Grandstand

Iowa FFA members Kelcy Cowan of Gladbrook and Ali Carlson of Columbus Junction are patrolling **SECTION "X"** of the Grandstand, which is on the west end of the grandstand seating. Every year, FFA members from across the state help ticket holders find their seats during grandstand events. Seating in the Grandstand is divided in Sections A-Z, with the MN section being in the center. There are also stage section seating, which consists of folding chairs, handicapped seating and bleachers. Altogether, there are 10,479 seats available during grandstand events. At almost 600 feet, the Grandstand is one of the largest buildings on the fairgrounds. On the side facing the Grand Concourse, there is exhibit space known as Shoppers' Mart which is in operation during the fair.

YE OLD MILL

Curt and Dotty Bates of Deep River, Iowa along with their daughter, Taren and her fiance, Austin Young, prepare for their ride on the **YE OLD MILL**. The tunnel of love was built in 1921 and completely rebuilt in 1996. For many fairgoers, a ride with their sweetheart on the Ye Old Mill is a yearly tradition.

YODELING

Laura McCargar, 8, of Pleasant Hill, Iowa tied with Larry Whitehill of Nevada, Iowa for first place in the **YODELING** contest. Yodeling, whistling and children's singing contests were all part of the Rural Americana Olde Tyme Competitions held in Pioneer Hall.

<u>ZUCCHINI</u>

There are two different **ZUCCHINI** competition classes in the Agriculture Building at the Iowa State Fair – open class and 4-H. Pictured are the entries in the 4-H Horticulture Show, garden crops division. In order to enter, youth going into grade 6 through recent high school graduates have to be in good standing with their enrollment report in the county extension office. If your child is interested in joining 4-H, please contact your local county extension office or check out www.iowa4hfoundation.org.

Z

ZEBRAS at the ZOO

Two black and white **ZEBRAS**
Living in the petting **ZOO**
Anxiously wait for next year's Iowa State Fair
Just like me and you!

State Fair Trivia

How much do you know about the Iowa State Fair? We have included 15 pictures of places or things - some are relatively easy and some are a little harder. Gather a group of friends and see if you can answer all of our trivia questions. Visit www.ourfrontporchbooks.com or send a SASE to Our Front Porch Books, P.O. Box 902, Montezuma, IA 50171 for the answers.

Fairground Brain Teasers

1 - Approximately 160 acres make up the campgrounds. Do you know which gates lead into the campgrounds from the fairgrounds? (**Bonus:** Which gate is nearest to the campers shown?)

2 - Grrr! These lions are located between two stages at the fairgrounds. What are they?

3 - Where is this farm tractor located?

State Fair Trivia

5 - What building is this?

6 - (Above) What are these and where are they housed?

7 - (Left) Where can you find this?

4 - The best seat at the fairgrounds is carved out near what building?

**Check out
www.ourfrontporchbooks.com
for the answers**

State Fair Trivia

9 - For as little as $75, you can leave your mark while helping renovate the fairgrounds. Bricks like these are placed in 14 different locations around the fairgrounds. Can you name at least seven of the locations? (**Bonus:** In which location are the bricks pictured found?)

8 - Clinton Mickles, 7, of Eddyville, Iowa is 'pumping' water in front of what building?

11 - Every year, long lines form as hungry fairgoers wait for free samples of Iowa foods. Which building do you have to visit to find the free food?

10 - Giant tenderloins are one of the many delicious foods found at various vendor booths on the fairgrounds. What vendor booth sports this sign?

State Fair Trivia

12 - Where are this sheep and lamb resting?

13 - This steer keeps watch of what building?

GAMMON BARN MUSEUM

14 - What is housed in this building?

15 - Where is this rooster hiding?

BRAIN TEASERS

ABOUT THE AUTHORS

Debbie Tindle Parker has had several works - including fiction, non-fiction and poetry - published in *Julien's Journal*, a regional magazine based in Dubuque, Iowa. She is a graduate of Montezuma High School and Central College in Pella, Iowa and has written several romance/mystery novels. Debbie has been camping at and attending the Iowa State Fair for more than 30 years. The fair is near and dear to her heart and making this book has been a dream come true.

J.O. Parker, a native of Tulsa, Okla., graduated from the University of Missouri - Columbia with a degree in agricultural journalism. He is the managing editor of *The Montezuma Republican* and *Brooklyn Chronicle* and has won numerous awards for his photography and writing. In 2003, he was chosen to participate in the Missouri Photo Workshop, and was awarded the Montezuma FFA Blue and Gold award. He was chosen as the 2004 Poweshiek County Friend of 4-H.

Debbie and J.O. first met in the campgrounds of the Iowa State Fair in 2003 while J.O. was doing a story on campers from the Montezuma, Iowa area. They dated and were engaged in May, 2004 and married in September of the same year. They reside in Montezuma, Iowa and are currently preparing to begin working on their next photography book, which will highlight Iowa towns using an ABC format.

THANKS & DEDICATION

Many people have helped turn our dream of doing this book into reality. We would like to thank Gary Slater, the Iowa State Fair Board, Lori Chappell and the marketing department staff, everyone who allowed us to capture their moments at the fair, Christian Photo, Holly McQueen, Greg Latza, Dennis Murphy, Dave Sutherland, Dan Gray and the Sutherland Printing staff, Roger Allen and Marge "Frau" Hall.

Debbie would like to dedicate this book to: Angie (Goeke) Hubbard, who spent many hours with me exploring, shopping, laughing, dreaming and searching the fairgrounds; Brenda Boots, who embraced my fair traditions and rituals; and all of the performers and entertainers who allowed me to ask questions and step into their worlds, especially Ernie Renn and the Shotgun Red Band who encouraged my friends and me to go to college.

I would like to dedicate this book to and extend a special thank you to: my brother, Jeff, for being my protector during my younger years while at the fair, putting up with my friends when we took over the camper and for always fixing, bringing and maintaining the camper; his wife, Megan, and her family, who are also our fair family; my nephews, Gavin and Sawyer for being such cute models – may they carry on the state fair camping tradition; my mother, Carole, for taking me camping when I was young and allowing my friends to stay with me from my teen years on and for her financial and emotional support; my cat, Squirt, who waited impatiently at home while I was at the fair and missed me while I was gone.

I would also like to thank Natalie Reidford, Jenni Sheppard, Emily Cook, Benae Duff, Mae Foster, Mary Stark, Mr. Rich Majerus and all of my friends and family who believed in my desire to see my words in print.

To my husband – you amaze me everyday. Thank you for turning all of my dreams into reality. I love you with all of my heart.